Governance of Co-owned Projects

Association for Project Management

Association for Project Management
Ibis House, Regent Park
Summerleys Road, Princes Risborough
Buckinghamshire
HP27 9LE

British Library Cataloguing in Publication Data is available.
Paperback ISBN: 978-1-903494-56-1
eISBN: 978-1-903494-57-8

Contents

Foreword

Many large, complex projects cut across organisational structures that work for organisations when they are in 'business-as-usual' mode – project success requires multiple organisations to voluntarily collaborate and work together in the interests of delivering the project, and therefore to not focus solely on their organisational interests.

There are of course, numerous benefits that can arise from organisations jointly working on projects – such as capitalising on complementary assets and skills, sharing costs and resources, diluting risk, and learning from the good (and bad) practices of others. It is however inherent that joint working means more than one organisation has the right to make decisions that affect the project as a whole, and so no single organisation has exclusive control. Such projects are deemed to be co-owned, and it is the challenge of how to govern the project in such circumstances, to the satisfaction of different boards, that this guide attempts to answer.

I have had the privilege of working on a number of complex yet successful programmes – including both the London 2012 Games, and delivering the long term legacy from them – which can be regarded as co-owned. When we established the governance arrangements for 2012 we could not apply traditional project governance approaches as they generally assume a single sponsor/owner and therefore would not adequately address co-ownership. Significant time, effort and indeed trial and error went into setting up and refining the governance arrangements to address the complexities that co-ownership brings. This guide would have helped our journey and I am sure will help others facing similar challenges.

This guide is succinct and is helpful to boards and their advisors by providing a set of underlying principles and associated considerations that can be assessed and applied.

David Goldstone CBE
Chief executive
London Legacy Development Corporation

Acknowledgements

This guide was developed by the Governance Specific Interest Group (SIG) of the Association for Project Management through workshops and working groups in 2015 and 2016, and is based on the original *Co-Directing Change* text, published in 2007. A special mention should go to the editorial panel of the 2007 version – Dr Hartley Millar, Martin Hopkinson, David Shannon and Peter Parkes.

Authoring group

Dr Hartley Millar, lead author, hartley@managementpartners.eu
Andy Murray, sponsor and contributor, andy.murray@rsmuk.com
Steve Jarrett, project manager, steve.jarrett@rsmuk.com

Contributors and reviewers

The authoring group express their thanks to all those who contributed to or reviewed these guidelines.

Alan Couzens	Ivan Stone	Ole Jonny Klakegg
Alistair Godbold	Jon Caton	Paul Watkins
Amerjit Walia	Jordi Ros	Peter Deary
Andrew Schuster	Julia Casson	Peter Hewitt
Andrew Spiers	Kevin Man	Roger Garrini
Arnab Banerjee	Martin Samphire	Simon Adams
Benedict Pinches	Margaret Onuora	Simon Henley
Brian Wernham	Mike Coker	Stephan Gehring
Dr David Broster	Mike Gill	Subash Tavares
Dr Roger Barker	Miles Dixon	Suzanne Davison
Emma-Jane Houghton	Mike Ward	Tony Czarnecki
Graeme Kyle	Nick Ashcroft	William Buist-Wells

The APM Governance SIG committee welcome suggestions for future editions of this guide and notifications of any errors.

1

Introduction

1.1 Context

The world today is increasingly interconnected. The role boundaries of government organisations, non-governmental organisations (NGOs), private enterprise, social enterprise, communities and individuals are increasingly ambiguous.

It is not surprising then that joint projects are becoming increasingly more common in practice. Whether it is government to government, government to NGO, government to private, private to private or any other form of joint project, the necessity and benefits of joint projects are leading to more organisations participating in more joint projects that are sometimes greater in scale and complexity than they have previously undertaken on their own.

By committing to a joint project the board of each participating organisation takes on more than if they did it on their own as each organisation will inevitably, in the eyes of stakeholders, be associated with the project – whether successful or not. So a core concept of joint projects is that they are 'co-owned' by the participating organisations.

The challenge for organisations who sponsor or deliver co-owned projects is that traditional project management frameworks and methods are based on governance structures that assume a single hierarchical route for authority and accountability. This is rarely the case for co-owned projects, which is why organisations are rightly challenging whether their traditional governance arrangements are fit for purpose.

1.2 Purpose

"How can boards be assured that their governance arrangements are appropriate for projects where they share control with other parties?"

The objective of this guide is to foster better practice in the governance of co-owned projects. It is aimed at those who influence corporate governance in organisations where the success of such projects is material to their performance. This includes members of company boards, company directors and executives, project portfolio directors, project sponsors, project managers and other professionals with key governance or assurance roles, such as legal, audit and financial specialists.

This guide is based on a set of principles to help establish the general governance arrangements for co-owned projects, and a set of key questions to prompt further specific context-based considerations. These principles and key questions can be used in two contexts:

- helping an organisation assess and/or establish or develop its corporate governance practice appropriate to being involved in co-owned projects (organisational governance);
- helping the co-owners of a joint project to assess and/or set up the governance arrangements for that specific project (project governance).

The way this guide can be used differs for these two contexts as outlined in the table below.

	Organisational governance	Project governance
What to assess	Reasons why any of the principles are not accepted – comply or explain. Validate using a sample of co-owned projects across the organisation.	The specific project in question only. Identify gaps and departures from the principles. Identify relevant key questions not satisfactorily answered.
Scope of assessment	The specific organisation only. Reviewing different types of co-owned projects experienced or likely to be considered.	Governance of the project by all the co-owners (and potential co-owners if desired).
How to use the results	Identify the corporate arrangements that need enhancing based on gaps identified.	Identify the specific arrangements for the project that need enhancing based on gaps identified.

Organisational governance	Project governance
Gaps may originate from: • exceptions and variability across the sample; • weak/absent organisational policies, guidance, capabilities or behaviours.	Gaps may originate from: • weak/absent arrangements within the project; • weak/absent corporate arrangements within the co-owning organisations.

When using these principles and key questions, boards will ideally want to ensure that their organisations' governance practices allow positive answers to all the key questions relevant to their co-owned projects. Using the list of key questions to assess a sample of projects should reveal underlying strengths and weaknesses the organisation has in general when undertaking co-owned projects.

In the case of a one-off involvement in a co-owned project, the set of key questions may also be valuable for organising and complementing normal due diligence and highlighting areas of potential risk. In this case, the focus should be on exploring the reasons why the answers to potentially relevant questions are negative or different among potential co-owners.

Use of this guide will help organisations proceed, with confidence, to maximise benefits from involvement in co-owned projects.

2

Principles for the governance of co-owned projects

Each co-owning board should strive to apply the following ten principles to its co-owned projects and evaluate the potential consequences where compromises need to be made.

These principles focus on factors relating to co-ownership rather than general factors relating to project management. For principles relating to the governance of project management generally, guidance can be found in the companion guides *Directing Change* and *Sponsoring Change*.

2.1 Formal arrangements

P01 Agreements

There should be formally agreed governance arrangements. These may include legal contracts and agreements among co-owners, which together ensure:

a. clear processes for decision making ensuring unified project management and unambiguous representation of each co-owner;
b. processes to deal with conflicts of duty, conflicts of interest, ambiguous accountability and the resolution of disputes;
c. explicit commitment to collaboration, resource provision, mobilisation and demobilisation.

P02 Flexibility and change management

The formal arrangements should provide for fundamental change including change in the group of co-owners and should define the process to be invoked. This includes changes as a result of revised project objectives or approach, resolution of conflicts, co-owners joining or leaving, or as a consequence of material change in control, relevant strategy or risk appetite within co-owning organisations.

P03 Benefits and rights

The formal arrangements should define the rights and responsibility for the realisation of benefits arising from the project and co-owners' obligations after leaving or on completion. They should include intangible benefits and the protection of co-owner's confidentiality and intellectual property, and rights to publicise outcomes or represent other co-owners.

2.2 Co-owner to co-owner due diligence

P04 Mutually-accepted business cases

Each co-owner should assure itself that each co-owner's organisation has a stable basis of internal approval of its business case for the project, and is committed to maximum openness about its nature and relevant changes as they may occur. Critical aspects of the business cases include clear definitions of project objectives, the role of each co-owner, their incentives and rewards, risk allocation, authority, commitment and responsibilities.

P05 Co-owners' legal and governance compatibility

Each co-owner should assure itself of the legal competence and relevant obligations of co-owners, and that internal governance arrangements of co-owners and any project delivery structure created are compatible with standards of governance acceptable to it.

P06 Co-owners' standing, culture and capability

Each co-owner should assure itself that co-owners' cultures, capabilities and reputation are appropriate to co-ownership of the project and also that co-owners' policies and practices on ethics and sustainability are acceptable to it.

2.3 Working arrangements

P07 Reporting

The depth, breadth and transparency of reporting should be fair, balanced and suitable for the audience to understand. Reports should provide the information needed for co-owners to make decisions, report onward to stakeholders and to trigger previously agreed independent review and corrective actions when they have legitimate concerns about the achievement of project objectives or viability.

P08 Assurance and transparency

Projects should incorporate arrangements for access to information necessary for co-owners' internal control or audit functions, for conformity with disclosure and transparency obligations, for independent assurance, and should also include channels for whistleblowing.

P09 Stakeholder relationships

There should be arrangements in place to ensure that the execution of projects takes account of co-owners' shareholder and other stakeholder relationships, and to deal with reputational risk and potential conflicts of interest.

P10 Trust, collaboration and value maximisation

There should be arrangements in place to build and maintain trust, collaboration and collaborative behaviour including identifying opportunities for improving the value of the project to co-owners.

3

Key questions for the governance of co-owned projects

This section offers key questions to help you explore and decide whether the principles of good governance are being followed. These questions can also be used to check the governance arrangements for an individual project.

3.1 Alignment and compatibility

These questions address the need for both formal and informal arrangements to ensure that there is sufficient mutual understanding and commitment, and that objectives and cultures, where different, are compatible.

Formal documentation is a fundamental strength in establishing co-ownership relations and its compatibility with the respective organisations' strategies needs to be clear and checked. However, by committing to co-owned projects each co-owner board must take account of more than is usually included in the formal documentation. Mutual understanding of strengths, weaknesses, cultures, ethics and strategies is essential to judging whether there is sufficient alignment or manageable complementarity amongst the co-owners to jointly and successfully address unforeseen challenges and opportunities. Also each co-owning organisation will inevitably be associated with the reputation and brand of the other co-owners and needs to take account of their characteristics and likely actions.

A01	Are the benefits, objectives and scope of the project: a. documented, understood and formally approved by all co-owners? b. consistent with each co-owner's strategic objectives?
A02	Have the contractual arrangements been scrutinised in each co-owning organisation by senior staff who are independent of the project and/or an external specialist, for gaps, ambiguities, unrecognised risks and oversights?

A03	Is each of the co-owners motivated for the project to succeed in delivering the collective outputs, outcomes and benefits, and not just the benefits to their own organisation?
A04	Have the key enablers for effective and efficient collaborative working and their implications been explored and understood by all co-owners?
A05	Has the need for a project identity, or 'branding' that is distinct from that of each co-owning organisation, been considered?
A06	Have co-owners' policies on issues such as ethics, culture and sustainability, and corporate responsibility been: a. reconciled? b. adopted by the project team?
A07	Have the co-owning organisations assessed and taken account of the other co-owners' relevant knowledge, strengths and competencies and those interests and relationships that might influence their contribution and commitment to the project?
A08	Is there an agreed and effective process documented and in place to manage changes to the project purpose, objectives or scope?
A09	Do the agreed strategies and mechanisms, including those for dispute resolution, foster trust amongst co-owning organisations?
A10	Is there a documented and agreed process in place to detect and attempt to deal with sources of conflict, such as attempted domination, changes in co-owners' strategies, risk appetite, performance or ownership and control?
A11	Are the processes for, and implications of, co-owners joining and leaving the project understood and agreed by all co-owners.
A12	Do the due diligence criteria for new joiners include commitment to good governance and evidence of compatibility?
A13	Have the co-owners created a process whereby agenda-setting and decision-making processes (e.g. majority, unanimity, escalation) are clear for different situations?
A14	Are agreed provisions and procedures in place for invoking external assistance for dispute avoidance, dispute resolution and support for a positive relationship among co-owners?

| A15 | Have the co-owners' agreements with and obligations to their suppliers, customers and other stakeholders been reconciled? |
| A16 | Is there clear agreement of how co-owners will, jointly or separately, explore new business opportunities outside the project scope but with contacts and/or stakeholders gained through the project? |

3.2 Reward, risk and opportunity

These questions focus on whether there is clarity about the principles and arrangements by which the potential rewards and opportunities for co-owners will be allocated and risks will be identified, allocated and mitigated in an integrated fashion.

Co-owned projects reward their co-owners in different ways, such as access to facilities or knowledge, market positioning, revenue from work on the project or thereafter, or capital growth. During the life of a project the risk/reward implications for co-owners may change, for example due to changes in ownership, or events within the project, or due to outside factors. Boards need to ensure an approach that is comprehensive and able to take account of the risk/reward strategies of co-owners, that balances risks and rewards and that triggers changes in reward and risk sufficiently early and with sufficient clarity.

R01	Have the risk appetites of the co-owners been openly reconciled, bearing in mind the project objectives, plan, benefits and areas of uncertainty?
R02	Is there an explicit listing of risks and opportunities for the project that includes mitigation strategies and clearly states which risks/impacts are to be carried singly by each co-owner and which are shared, including the basis of sharing?
R03	Are the ratio and relationships of reward to risk for each co-owner understood and agreed by the other co-owners, including how they may vary?
R04	Is there throughout the project a dependable and integrated process for identifying, assessing and allocating both risks and rewards in respect of the project and all co-owners?

R05	Does the process for allocating and addressing risk take account of the respective co-owners' expressed risk appetites and the time frames for action?
R06	Are project risk mitigation strategies regularly reviewed and contingencies regularly re-estimated, controlled and communicated to co-owners?
R07	Is there a clear and agreed realisation strategy that takes account of co-owners' potentially different priorities and trade-offs, e.g. between capital and income?
R08	Do agreements and measures exist to determine what constitutes early or late realisation of benefits or rewards?
R09	Are there agreements identifying and determining the sharing and realisation of benefits from intellectual property rights and other potential intangible benefits?
R10	Is there a mechanism in place for transferring rights to future benefits both in the case of transfer of ownership and amongst co-owners?
R11	Is it clear in the case of joiners/leavers and in the case of project termination how the rights, rewards, risks, opportunities, obligations and liabilities will be allocated to co-owners?
R12	Is reputational risk for co-owners identified and fully understood by the other co-owners and the project team?
R13	Is there a clear and agreed basis for reaching timely agreement on significant additional opportunities, e.g. potential exploitation or extension beyond the original scope?

3.3 Leadership and sponsorship

These questions seek to identify whether there is an effective link between the senior governing body of each co-owning organisation and the management of specific projects.

Cascading downwards from the board, leadership is a basic requirement of corporate governance, which affects, and should be reflected in, all projects including co-owned projects.

Such leadership is typically achieved through representatives of each co-owning organisation. These representatives, through their interaction with unified project management (Principle 1a), are the mechanism for ensuring that co-owned projects are effectively directed, operate according to agreed remits, transmit reports to each co-owner and obtain decisions from each co-owner board.

There may be circumstances where owning organisation representation is the collective responsibility of a group/client function or committee rather than being the responsibility of one individual; for convenience and readability, however, the questions that follow are phrased in terms of an individual serving as a 'co-owner representative'.

L01	Does each co-owning organisation appoint and ensure active ongoing engagement of a suitably qualified and experienced co-owner representative?
L02	Are the co-owner representatives' roles in their own organisations appropriate for ensuring that all aspects of their boards' accountability are catered for?
L03	Do the co-owner representatives, through their interaction with unified project management, provide and support effective leadership, sponsorship and direction?
L04	Do co-owner representatives promote, through being role models, collaboration and openness/transparency at all levels?
L05	Do co-owner representatives adequately represent and communicate the project throughout their own organisations? Are there formal channels for the representative to interact with, and obtain timely decisions from, the board?
L06	Do co-owner representatives meet each other and any independent non-executives of the project regularly (formally and informally) and maintain sufficient awareness of the project status and each others' views on this?
L07	Do all senior project participants have clear and agreed reporting relationships and delegated authority from their boards or co-owner representatives?
L08	Do co-owner representatives have the delegated authority to initiate processes for the project to be re-scoped, closed or participation to be reviewed?
L09	Do co-owner representatives protect the project team from undue interference by their own organisations?

L10	Do co-owner representatives recognise and understand any potential conflicts in statutory duties and have they taken advice (legal if necessary) to ensure conflicts are explicit or removed?
L11	Do co-owner representatives ensure accountability for the realisation of project benefits within their own organisations and for close-down of the project on completion?

3.4 Project management capability

Project success is closely correlated with the capabilities, competence and performance of the project team. Boards need to assure themselves that sufficient resources are put in place and pay special attention to ensuring that all those allocated roles in the project – from the board members down – are competent and empowered in the role that they are expected to undertake.

The questions focus most on those management and control areas that might be of particular concern in setting up governance arrangements for co-owned projects.

PM01	Are key project governance roles and responsibilities clear and in place – for the project and for each co-owner?
PM02	Is there a clearly documented and proven approach to the management of the project and the authority of the project management that all co-owners have agreed to and will abide by?
PM03	Is there a mutually approved plan for the committed stages of the project? Is it pragmatic, has it got sufficient contingency and does it include appropriate formal review points and their approval criteria, e.g. stage gates?
PM04	Are robust processes in place to ensure the full and timely availability of inputs (including resources) from co-owning organisations and for early warning of any potential shortfalls or substitutions?
PM05	Are the people responsible for project delivery clearly mandated, sufficiently competent and experienced, and sufficiently committed and available to achieve satisfactory project outcomes?

PM06	Are there arrangements to ensure that the project management methodologies to be used on the project are mutually agreed, understood and applied by all team members?
PM07	Are there specific measures in place to incentivise or drive 'one team' working and collaboration, and ensure that team members identify with the project and internalise its values and way of working?
PM08	Does the team understand and accept reputational sensitivity and the potential for project activities harming it and co-owners?
PM09	Are the working environments and employment conditions of team members from different organisations tailored so as to minimise discontent, friction and jealousy?
PM10	Has every effort been made to create optimal working conditions including, for example, co-location of the core project team?
PM11	Is there a robust system whereby team members' performance within the project is also recognised by their own organisation?

3.5 Disclosure and reporting

These questions highlight the need for the provision, sharing and use of information to support co-owners' evidence-based decision making without fostering a culture of micro management.

Good corporate governance requires the right level of information reported at the right time and in the right way, and co-owners should be able to instigate independent verification of information where appropriate. Creation of an 'arms length' vehicle for the delivery of a co-owned project does not remove the accountability of the respective boards for their investment and its success.

Assurance extends beyond the performance and reporting of the project itself; boards of co-owning organisations need to be confident that assurance is integrated, addresses the effectiveness of the inter-organisational arrangements and behaviours, and that, where necessary, the involvement of an independent assurance function is available.

Governance of Co-owned Projects

In the interests of both co-owners' compliance and the co-owned project itself, disclosure should be extended to all stakeholders to the extent that they have a legitimate interest in project information.

D01	Are co-owners and their representatives aware of their individual and other co-owners' corporate governance responsibilities for disclosure, transparency and reporting about the project?
D02	Does project reporting and disclosure provide the information necessary for each co-owner to respond to their organisation's stakeholders who wish to exercise their rights or responsibilities, such as under relevant Stewardship codes?
D03	Are the triggers that might lead to dispute, the halting of the project, alteration of its scope or the withdrawal of co-owners, clearly identified and covered in reports?
D04	Are mechanisms in place requiring co-owners to fully disclose to each other, as soon as their situation allows, information that may affect their participation, including changes in their own circumstances, positions or objectives?
D05	Is there agreement on measurement and reporting criteria for key performance parameters including time, cost, risk, benefits, quality and intangibles such as reputation?
D06	Do co-owners cooperate when appropriate to seek independent verification of project forecasts and reports?
D07	Are arrangements for agreed independent and integrated assurance at key stages of the project in place?
D08	Are channels and protection for whistle-blowers effective in both the management and the governance of the project?
D09	Are there arrangements to conduct post-project evaluations and to feed back 'lessons learnt' and share appropriate intellectual property among co-owners?

4

Further guidance

Many organisations are subject to codes of corporate governance related to how and where they were incorporated, such as the UK Corporate Governance Code for UK listed companies. There are also guides and standards relating to some aspects of the governance of co-owned projects, such as the BS11000 Collaborative Business Relationships.

The APM Governance Specific Interest Group has developed a set of supporting data-sheets showing how the principles and key questions in this guide relate to such codes, guides and standards. They are available to APM members via the APM website apm.org.uk/community/governance-sig.

Appendix – Terms

In this guide we use the words 'governance', 'project', 'co-owned' and 'board' as follows:

Governance
This guide follows the definition of governance of project management contained in the companion guide *Directing Change*, which is based upon principles of corporate governance developed by the Organisation for Economic Co-operation and Development (OECD) as 'a set of relationships between an organisation's owners, its board, its management and other stakeholders. This provides the structure through which the organisation's objectives are set and the means of attaining those objectives and of monitoring performance are determined.' It is also informed by the UK Corporate Governance Code, which has the principle of 'comply or explain' at its core.

The *Governance of Project Management* concerns those areas of corporate governance that arise from an organisation's project/change activities and require attention at board level. It should be distinguished from the *Governance of Individual Projects*, on the other hand, which concerns the specific governance arrangements for individual projects and programmes.

Project
A unique complex undertaking that delivers 'change' requiring the use of project or programme management methodology. The word 'project' in this context includes programmes of projects.

Co-owned
A project is co-owned if more than one organisation shares ultimate control over the decision-making process regarding fundamental aspects of the project such as purpose, objectives, scope, finance, resources, roles of participating organisations, or allocation of risks or benefits.

Governance of Co-owned Projects

Board

This applies to an organisation's board of directors and their equivalents in the public sector and to a governing council in companies limited by guarantee. It specifically **does not** refer to a project or programme board.

Governance of co-owned projects

Governance of co-owned projects refers to the relationships, objectives setting, decision-making, behaviour and reporting arrangements that must be established such that the board of each co-owner can be assured that governance responsibilities will be met when it takes part in a co-owned project.

As depicted below the corporate governance responsibilities of co-owning organisations include governance of project management in their own organisations and hence there is an overlap in their respective responsibilities for governance of the co-owned project.

Organisation 1 governance   Organisation 2 governance

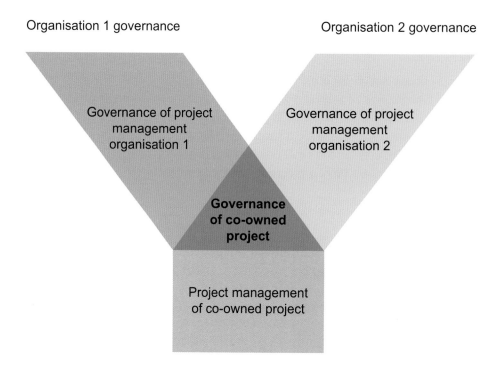

Governance of project management organisation 1

Governance of project management organisation 2

Governance of co-owned project

Project management of co-owned project

Corporate governance issues arising from project management within organisations are addressed by the principles set out in the companion guide *Directing Change*. These also apply when the organisation participates in a co-owned project; the focus of this guide is on additional issues and on areas of particular vulnerability or concern that arise in the case of co-ownership. Similarly, the other companion guide *Sponsoring Change* is also relevant to the sponsors of a co-owned project. Both should be read in conjunction with this guide.